Gently George

Helen Griffiths

Gently George

Copyright © *Helen,* 2025
All Rights Reserved

To George,

My inspiration and purest joy

Lots of love

Nana

Little George was a lucky boy
With lots of toys and games
He liked playing in a cardboard box
Which he used as a house or a plane

George loved his mummy
And his daddy too
He enjoyed playing games
Like chase and peekaboo!

But his favourite thing
Which made him feel giggly
Was his black and white cat
And her name was Tilly

George got so excited
To see his little cat
That he'd jump up and run over
To have a friendly chat

George running so fast
Meant Tilly ran away
As it made her feel frightened
And she didn't want to play

So George walked to see Tilly
And he was quite slow
Then Tilly felt better
And she didn't rush to go

But George got excited
He wasn't going to stop
When he touched her soft fur
His hand closed up

Tilly let out a 'meow'
His grip was far too tight
She felt scared and unhappy
And again ran away in fright

Mummy said to George
"I know you love Tilly so,
You've got to be very gentle
Then she won't want to go"

Daddy sat down with George
To show how to stroke Tilly's head
How his hand and fingers stayed open
So she felt safe and happy instead

When George knew what to do
And was gentle with his cat
Tilly started to feel safe with him
And she'd fall peacefully asleep in his lap

When George plays in his cardboard box
Tilly jumps in, eyes open wide
George and Tilly are the best of friends,
And play happily side by side